SIMPLY BE YOUR MAGNIFICENT SELF!

A Guide for Empowering Girls and Women

To Debby,

Paving the way for
two magnificent girls & a
wise son.
Enjoy!

Cindy Stauffer
December 2016

Simply Be Your Magnificent Self!

A Guide for Empowering Girls and Women

by

Donna R. Styer

and

Cynthia Stauffer

Foreword by Carrie Johnson

Printed in the United States of America

First Printing, 2016

ISBN: 978-0-692-77113-6

Published by D. R. Styer and C. C. Stauffer

For my sons, Steven and Jason,
with great love and admiration.
~D.S.

For my beloved sister by marriage, Debbie Campbell, who
has demonstrated to her children the values of honesty, hard
work, loyalty, optimism, perseverance, and integrity.
~C.S.

Acknowledgments

We sincerely thank the many people who helped to bring this book to completion. We are grateful to the interviewees who shared their stories and pieces of their past with honesty and emotion. Some of the interviewees were: Shelby Nauman; Laura Howell; Vicki Philips; Janette Hewitt; Barbara Eberly; Casey Dixon; Jo Tyler; Cyndi Beyerline; Leigh Hurst; Denise Bray; Steven, Dawn, Courtney, Kaila, Kara, and Kirstin Funk; Jane Hoover; Trisha Robinson; Amy and Lisa Malehorn; Linda Hopple; Alicia Richards; Bobbi Carmitchell; Joan Todd; Doreen Landis; Annie Carmitchell; Conni Shertzer; Jason and Nicole Funk; Deenie Rose; Michael, Andrea, and Jenna Styer; Jessica Smucker; Wynne Kinder; Leigh Wisotsky; Abby Hennesy-Withum; Rebecca Margerum; Robena Spangler; Susan Moore; and Lisa Heycock. For any interviewees whose names were overlooked, please know we are sincerely grateful for your time and for sharing.

In addition to the interviewees were over 1,000 individuals who took time to complete our survey—thank you!

We gratefully acknowledge the talented individuals who provided editorial assistance along the way. Dr. Kerry Sherin Wright got us back on track with her simple words of wisdom so that the show (or book) could go on! And many, many thanks to Dr. Wright for directing us to our wonderful editor, Delphine Martin. Thanks also to Kathryn Wanner and Lauren Cusick for their editorial guidance and organization earlier in the project, and to Sherwood Stauffer for his patience and guidance, especially when we needed help with organization.

Our heartfelt thanks go to Freiman Stoltzfus, an incredible artist, for creating our lovely cover art and design! Also, a very special thank-you to Carrie Johnson for simply being her fabulous self and for writing the foreword. Her magnificence shines!

We greatly appreciate Susan Pera, who let us claim "our table" at her Cornerstone Café in Camp Hill, hour after hour, week after week. Her kindness and patience allowed us to write a huge part of the book in her fabulous café.

A Special thank you to the great team at North Market Street Graphics! Especially Vicky Dawes, Lainey Wolfe and Mark Righter. You were so committed, supportive and professional. It was my pleasure to work with all of you!

We also sincerely thank our clients for the privilege of sharing in their lives. What a gift they are to us!

Finally, we are grateful to all those who were or are in our lives—all our family and friends—who helped us become the women we are today. Their love and understanding is food for our souls. A heartfelt thank-you—we are blessed!

Donna Styer and Cindy Stauffer

Table of Contents

Contents

Foreword

When we brought each of our daughters home from the hospital, I remember wishing for a "how to" manual. After all, women have been having babies for centuries. Surely there must be a book I can read that will tell me how to coach them and navigate through their years ahead, to set them on the path to confidence, right?

Simply Be Your Magnificent Self! A Guide for Empowering Girls and Women is that tidy toolkit we all can carry with us through life to help empower our girls, friends, and ourselves. The beauty of this book is that it spans generations and genders.

When placed in the hands of its readers, it will change lives and help build the foundation for girls and women to value and celebrate their strengths, activate their power, and share their voices.

This book is a call to action for all of us because

our girls matter, and investing in their limitless potential and our collective bright futures is one of the most powerful legacies we can leave. We all share a sense of responsibility to leave this world better than when we arrived. By using this book as a tool to help our girls realize their gifts and become the "bosses of their own brains," and also by putting it into the hands of the ones who love girls and women, we have changed the world.

Thank you, Donna and Cindy, for your tireless hearts and hands!

Carrie Johnson
Executive Director, Girls on the Run of Lancaster
Mom of two teenage girls

Introduction

Simply Be Your Magnificent Self! is a book written by two women with very different backgrounds and separate careers who found one another by mere happenstance at a drumming event, at different life phases. From there, the authors grew to appreciate their mutual passion for the topic of girls' and women's self-esteem and authenticity.

The desire to write this book arose out of our shared professional and personal experiences with women and girls. We encountered females of all ages who were struggling with self-esteem issues and needed guidance on how to care for themselves. We were especially struck by the negative ways young girls viewed themselves and the world and how those perceptions affected their self-esteem and confidence. In essence, we wanted to create a way to encourage others to begin helping girls, as *early* as possible, in developing courage, confidence, and authenticity.

The ideas that molded this book come from many sources, including each author's life experience. Cynthia Stauffer is a child psychologist and mother of three young women. Donna Styer is a professional coach specializing in executive, career, and life coaching, and the mother of two sons.

We honor the hundreds of women who shared their joys and sorrows with us. We interviewed more than 100 women from all walks of life (and a number of men), and their stories are woven into this book. We also included information from over 1,000 women surveyed on their perceptions of childhood influences that helped them blossom. All of these individuals contributed to the development of this practical guide.

Simply Be Your Magnificent Self! highlights ways to cultivate extraordinary personal growth in girls throughout their life span. The easy-to-follow suggestions in nine areas enable you to lovingly guide them into being their authentic selves and positively impact their development. You will be made aware of the importance of *mindfully* applying simple changes in how you talk to them, how to help them navigate life's challenges, and how to foster the confidence to be the people they would like to be. You will find ways to use positive guidance and affirmation, both of which strengthen their potential to make wise choices. Hopefully this book will enlighten you and compel you to grow in ways you never dreamed.

In the first chapter, the writers bring awareness to some of the ways society inhibits the healthy development of girls. The remainder of the book offers easy-to-follow strategies to help females flourish and overcome those challenges. These include sensible suggestions on nine different topics: subliminal messages/double standards, authenticity, communication, self-discipline, independence, nurturance, boundaries, humor, and friendship.

The ideas presented in *Simply Be Your Magnificent Self!* are straightforward and relatively easy to implement. You may begin applying some of these ideas with young girls, teens, or *yourself.* You may choose to read the book from cover to cover or select chapters according to your area of interest. Fortunately, increasing your awareness in any one of the topics presented could help you to effect positive change in the girl you love and may even benefit your own growth.

Virtually anyone may benefit from the information offered. You may be a parent, teacher, neighbor, or grandparent or someone coming into regular contact with girls. If you are a mature reader, we hope you will discover new insights into womanhood that will help you realize more personal satisfaction and joy. In many of the chapters, you can replace "girl" with "woman" and apply the suggestions to your own life. You will be pleasantly surprised at what you may learn about yourself in the process!

We promise you inspiration and joy as you learn more about girlhood and as you and the girls you love become the magnificent women you were born to be!

1

Subliminal Messages and Double Standards

"We can't control the wind, but we can control our sails."
—Anonymous

Girls begin life quite innocently. They see a dandelion as a flower, pick a bunch for their teachers, and feel good. They know as youngsters that they are beautiful just the way they are. But what happens after that? What makes an eight-year-old girl decide that life is unfair for girls? Why do so many girls strive to be someone other than who they are? And why do seven out of ten girls believe their looks, their weight, or their performance are not good enough?

For answers to these questions, it is helpful to look at some of our long-held gender beliefs. For instance, on a radio show one man was asked about the differences in raising boys versus girls. This man discussed raising his son to be strong and productive while referring to his daughter as his "little princess." This chapter discusses subliminal messages, such as this one, that our girls may receive. In being aware of these messages, they can overcome them and thrive.

Subliminal messages are any messages that have hidden meanings. In this chapter we are referring to messages girls receive about what it means to be a female in our society. Subliminal messages can take many forms. For example, they can be stereotypes. If a girl hears the phrase "You throw like a girl," she receives the message that girls are not as strong as boys. Subliminal messages can also come from media, politics, sports, or any aspect of our culture. If there are few strong female role models in politics or positions of power, girls may receive the message that these opportunities do not exist for them. Subliminal messages can also be messages that girls receive in commercials and television about what it means to be beautiful as a woman. These messages come from many places and are a serious barrier for girls to achieve their true potential.

We want to help you, the reader, to be more mindful of the beliefs you hold and the messages you may be sending to the girls in your lives through your words and choices. In this book we offer intentional practices and statements that work to overcome the countless negative subliminal messages in society.

Boys and girls, as children, have many of the same needs, but some aspects of girls' development require unique attention. Girls are profoundly impacted by what they see in the media. For example, many images of women in magazines are airbrushed, leading many girls to develop an unrealistic image of what real women look like. There are also many depictions of violence against women in the media to which young girls may be exposed. This has many negative consequences for women and girls, such as a feeling of not being safe, or even that this violence is acceptable.

Young girls are especially susceptible to conventional beliefs about female roles. This vulnerability can prevent them from considering other options for themselves or prevent them from pursuing leadership positions. We were surprised to learn that a woman's image has not been featured on paper money in the United States in over a hundred years. In 1896, Martha Washington was the first woman to be featured on a silver certificate. That means that for over one hundred years, girls have been given the message that women are not worthy of that recognition. Once again, a woman's image may finally be printed on paper money, but we think one hundred years is way too long.

Subliminal messages about opportunities for girls are heard in many aspects of society. Following are some related statistics for your reference. We invite you to consider these examples and reflect on how they might affect the girls and women in your lives.

Sports

- Men are vastly overrepresented in sporting events in the media. If a girl is looking to find a female sporting event on television, she is hard-pressed to find one.

- The average NBA player makes $4.9 million. Female counterparts in the

WNBA make an average of $72,000
and their salaries are capped at $105,000
(Racine 2015).

- An overwhelming majority of pictures
  in the sports pages show male athletes, so
  sometimes we have to wonder, Are there
  female athletes?

- The prize purse for winning the
  FIFA Women's World Cup in 2015 was
  $15 million compared to $358 million
  that was awarded to the men's team in 2014
  (Racine 2015).

Professional

- Women comprise only 5% of Fortune 500
  Chief Executive Officers (Lindzon 2015).

- The United States has never had a female
  president. Women hold 19% of the seats in
  the House of Representatives and 20% of

the seats in the Senate despite comprising 51% of the population (Lindzon 2015).

* Women made only 78 cents on the dollar as compared to men in 2015. In 2009, the Lilly Ledbetter Fair Pay Act clarified that each discriminatory paycheck is a new act of discrimination (Catalyst).

Media

* Women hold only 5% of leadership positions in mainstream media (*Miss Representation* 2011).

* Women comprised 9% of directors and 15% of film writers in the 250 top-grossing films of 2012 (*Miss Representation* 2011).

* Among 13-year-old girls, 53% are unhappy with their bodies. By age 15, that percentage increases to 78% (*Miss Representation* 2011).

* The number of cosmetic surgical procedures performed on 17-year-old girls tripled from 1997–2007. In the same ten-year period, liposuction nearly quadrupled and breast augmentation increased six-fold (*Miss Representation* 2011).

* Women represent 82% of the buying power (*Miss Representation* 2011).

Despite the fact that women have come a long way, a double standard still exists in society. Females are often held to higher or different standards than males in many aspects of life. For example, men who state clearly what they want, expect, or need are viewed as assertive, but even today, women who do the same are often called condescending names. Women are scrutinized for the way they look, such as mothers being criticized for not losing their pregnancy weight fast enough, or women being assessed for their attire on a daily basis or on the red carpet. We think that the best way to deal with some of these double standards is to be aware of them and continue to foster skills of courage and confidence in our girls that help them to combat these messages. Conversations with your girl about these double standards can be extremely helpful.

Beyond the statistics, the emotional reactions of the women we interviewed helped us to further underscore the impact of early life messages upon the developing female well into adulthood. The women we encountered gave us a deeper understanding of how these influences carried into their personal lives and their workplaces. We realized many women lacked awareness of their capability to lead and forge ahead, in the work world and in their relationships. Many were quick to dismiss their personal accomplishments and positive traits for fear of being viewed as bragging.

Fortunately, positive changes are occurring within our country. More and more women are running for public office and winning. Females are gaining confidence in pursuing leadership positions in the workplace. Women, in general, are more aware of the importance of gaining positive self-esteem through courage, confidence, and authenticity, and are creating wonderful organizations to enhance girls' and women's lives. (At the end of this book, we highlight some of the great organizations working for girls.) Still, we have a long way to go.

So what do we do with this information? In the following chapters, we offer suggestions to help combat these messages that girls are receiving. Much of what we share relates to helping girls develop the degree of self-confidence and -esteem needed to move forward and pursue their life goals. Positive self-esteem, or a favorable appreciation of one's self-image, leads to great things. With positive self-esteem, girls can build independence, avoid self-blame, and express positive and negative emotions in a healthy way. And we know that when women's self-esteem increases, so do the harmony, confidence, assertiveness, and fulfillment in their relationships.

Clearly, parents' words and actions play a major role in influencing girls' self-esteem. Parents may teach girls to effectively interpret the messages they receive in their early years. In so doing, they encourage independence, critical thinking, and authenticity.

"I am not afraid of storms, for I am learning how to sail my ship."

—Louisa May Alcott

2

Authenticity

*"Tell me, what is it you plan to do with your one
wild and precious life?"*
—Mary Oliver

Authenticity for girls is foundational to their development. This will be more evident as the book progresses. This particular chapter focuses on the critical need to give girls the freedom to develop a strong sense of who they are early on so they may pursue their true selves.

The authentic female is real, not false. She is comfortable with who she chooses to be. She lives what she believes, values, thinks, and feels without being contaminated by social stereotypes and what others expect of her. She freely expresses her creativity without fear of being judged and is genuine in relationships. In essence, authenticity is the ability to be true to yourself and live your most honest life.

How many of us marvel at the innocence of young girls as they freely express their wishes and dreams for the future? We listen to and watch them with admiration while they are still freshly viewing themselves, still free from stereotypes or expectations about what others think they should be, think, or do. We have heard young girls excitedly profess their wish to be famous poets, aspire to help those in need, or vow to feed all the hungry people in the world. Imagine even one young girl being encouraged to stay on track and lead the world in one of her dreams, perhaps eliminating hunger!

Girls' dreams blossom when they are encouraged to be true to themselves—to express their authenticity. When girls and women learn to express what they truly think and feel, and become who they want to be, they move toward a greater sense of well-being. Further, the ability to practice being authentic or true in relationships brings about a greater sense of harmony when in the company of others.

So often girls aspire to be more like someone else—certain celebrities, models, or musicians— rather than taking a unique and authentic path to their futures. We propose that while admiration of others is perfectly healthy, all too often the developing girl leaves her dreams behind to become what others want her to be or to be like her favorite celebrity rather than her authentic self.

We all know girls with strong opinions about dressing themselves unconventionally or behaving in unexpected ways. And certainly, we have observed firsthand how those girls are often criticized and scorned. For instance, one girl came to counseling for behavioral problems and in the course of therapy talked about her love of fishing. She beamed when describing her solitary jaunts to the local creek to fish. She, however, was acutely aware of her difficulty fitting in with other girls who didn't share her interest in fishing and who perceived her as odd. Over time, the effect of bullying took its toll and her self-esteem suffered. This is not an unusual scenario. Girls are often referred to counseling for similar difficulties—mainly because they feel sad and alone after being bullied and criticized by their peers for being "different." All too often, bullying is also related to their appearance if it doesn't measure up to societal standards.

Girls are increasingly concerned with their appearance and how they fit in—as early as kindergarten. We hear girls self-evaluating their appearance and weight. Do we really want our girls to grow up believing they need to meet standards that most of them will never be able to achieve? Do we want them to accept the appearance of models in magazines as authentic?

Advertisements convince many females to alter their appearance and reject their natural beauty. These messages are inescapable and widespread—on billboards, on television shows, in movies, and in advertising. Few can dispute their negative influence on girls and women. Left alone to view these messages without adult input, the developing girl is vulnerable to their impact. This is why it is crucial to discuss with young girls that commercials are geared toward getting them to buy things. It is all about the money!

Many girls are tricked into believing that their physical appearance is directly linked to their worthiness, so it's no surprise that their self-esteem is strongly related to how they view their appearance. One respondent sadly commented that she always thought she was judged by her size rather than by her intelligence.

Indeed, women we spoke to tended to evaluate their self-worth by their appearance. One interview respondent said what she wanted to change most about herself was her face and wrinkles. Others commented on their weight. How many of you have ever heard a man ask, "Do these pants make my butt look big?" This collective desire of many women to change their appearance fuels our economy. Females are compelled to lengthen lashes, tuck tummies, enlarge breasts, darken skin, paint nails, hide gray, inject Botox, whiten teeth, remove hair, and lose weight.

Parents can deeply influence girls' paths to authenticity and lessen the powerful influence of the media. Again, conversation is important to help girls decipher these influences. Looking back at their childhoods, a high percentage of women we surveyed wished their parents had more readily conveyed to them a sincere *acceptance* and *appreciation* for their uniqueness as children. Many of them believed their natural talents and interests went unnoticed in their parents' quest to teach them right from wrong. And while many of them as young girls were introduced to a variety of opportunities, sometimes they were involved in activities more closely mirroring their parents' interests than their own.

Another way that adults can encourage authenticity in girls is to encourage their curiosity. Some adults question their career choices long after they have invested years of time, money, and energy into a particular line of work. On reflection, they admit to never really having enjoyed their work or their life choices. Children are molded by life experiences and the messages they receive. Decisions about careers or other life choices are too often externally rather than internally driven. That is, girls often depend upon adults to make choices for them, when, in fact, the girls' innate desires need to be listened to and discussed.

Some interview respondents expressed regret that, while making life choices, they focused too much on making others happy and too little on their own aspirations. If more people in their lives had encouraged authenticity, they may have been better able to trust their instincts and follow their dreams. They may have been less likely to pursue a profession or lifestyle outside of their comfort zone. Career coaches often advocate that people try to stay in their passion zone. This provides the best chance for daily fulfillment, and, typically, people are good at what they love to do.

A girl who spends her childhood cultivating her own interests is more likely to find satisfaction and meaning in a career. She who celebrates her authenticity is on the road to positive self-esteem. Women who feel good about themselves and what they are doing are healthier and happier.

Part of the challenge in encouraging authenticity is shifting the manner in which messages are delivered. As role models to our girls, we must work extra hard to undo the effects of the negative influences from our culture and the media so our girls may pursue their dreams and become their *authentic selves*—who they truly are. Helping girls to identify sources of pride and teaching them to praise themselves will provide them with skills they can take into adulthood. Those who are encouraged, "Feel good about yourself," rather than "I am proud of you," will learn to evaluate and praise their own accomplishments rather than wait for someone else to do it for them. Of course it is acceptable for adults to express pride in young girls, but the more important message is that girls should internalize their own sense of accomplishment. When the emphasis is on getting adult praise, a girl learns to focus on pleasing adults. Rather than pursuing her desired goals, she gets derailed onto the path of living for others. She needs to find *comfort* and *fulfillment* in creating balance between living for herself and living for others.

Meryl Streep, in a 2010 commencement address at Barnard College, Columbia University, discussed her own meandering path to authenticity. She shared how in high school she adjusted her high-spirited personality to be more sweet and shy in order to appeal to boys. These are some of the ways girls learn to censor their true selves to meet the expectations of others. (Streep's full speech is available on YouTube.)

The authentic female, depending on her age, adopts her own style, knows who she is, feels good about who she is, knows her interests, lives life the way she wants to, and is grateful for the body she has. She is pleased with who she is, despite the way the media or others dictate. And the authentic girl will be less tempted to succumb to media influences. Also, she will be more of a risk taker.

Simple changes in long-held approaches to influencing girls may truly help to *foster authenticity*. Imagine every child learning to welcome diversity and to respect the opinions and choices of his or her peers! Further, imagine a girl being celebrated for her unique ways or praised for her efforts more than her accomplishments. These are all paths to authenticity!

Ways to Encourage Authenticity:

* Model how to respect and value people regardless of the color of their skin, their physical abilities, the language they speak, or their culture.

* Let her take age-appropriate risk. For example, grant her some independence to make decisions about her attire, when appropriate, and celebrate her clothing choices as expressions of her authenticity.

- Provide plenty of opportunities for her to experience the arts, nature, athletics, drama, and education to broaden her worldview.

- Counter her negative self-statements, such as "I am ugly" or "My legs are too fat," with questions about her interests and accomplishments.

- Teach her to be grateful for her body and appreciate all that it can do.

- Teach her to practice positive self-talk that offers encouragement and praise, such as "I feel proud of what I accomplished."

- Celebrate her unique talents and efforts. Offer to introduce her to others who share her talents or interests.

- Have interactive conversations about these topics, ask lots of questions, and deeply listen to her answers.

- Teach her to adopt gratitude for who she is and all of her gifts.

- Ask questions to enhance her critical thinking, and actively listen to her answers.

- Expect and encourage her to have questions and comments.

- Focus on her strengths and internal beauty rather than on her physical appearance.

- Spend time getting to know what she wants and loves.

- Comment on advertisements as they occur. Have conversations about this!

- Love her for who she is, celebrate her *uniqueness*, and *accept her being*.

- Respect all girls and women.

- Give her your undivided attention when having a conversation.

- Show her unconditional love.

- Let her know that you believe in her.

◇◇◇◇◇◇◇◇◇◇◇

"It's so important to be yourself, because everyone else is taken."

—OSCAR WILDE

◇◇◇◇◇◇◇◇◇◇◇

3

Communication

"There are two ways of spreading the light, to be a candle or the mirror that reflects it."
—EDITH WHARTON

Healthy communication is a major contributor to positive self-esteem and meaningful relationships. Girls who believe they are heard and understood are often self-confident. Further, they tend to be better communicators. They are also more willing to spend time with their parents, mentors, or caregivers when they can communicate freely and easily with them. Thus, it may come as no surprise that we devote a chapter of this book to communication. Communication, in the broadest sense, is the exchange of thoughts, information, or messages. When one thinks of the term "communication," the first thing that comes to mind is probably conversation.

Good communication has some basic requirements, including active listening and language that can be understood by the listener. For starters, the best way parents and caregivers can foster good communication is through actively listening. That is, they show true interest in hearing what she is saying, look in her eyes, and respond to what is being said. Therapists teach parents to express an understanding of what their children are trying to say by repeating back what they heard and by asking clarifying questions. Asking questions shows interest and conveys respect for what is being said.

Modeling good communication lays a foundation for girls to practice it themselves. Showing a desire to understand the meaning behind what girls are saying and making eye contact with them conveys interest. One of our survey respondents said she wished her mother had paid more attention to her bad report card! A study by the Dove Foundation found that one of the top wishes among girls is for their parents to communicate better with them and have more frequent and open conversations about what is happening in their own lives ("Real girls, real pressure").

Consider this all too common scenario: A girl stands at the bus stop day after day while her parent talks on a cell phone. As time goes on, the child comes to believe that what she has to say is less significant than her parent's phone conversation. As dependence on technology has increased in recent years, parents have become more and more likely to inadvertently ignore their children during important moments. Parents talk on their phones while pushing baby strollers or driving their children to and from events. The message these parents may unknowingly convey to a child is: "You matter less than my phone." While many parents are engaged on their cell phones, many children are left to feel unimportant.

Adults can do much to open lines of communication. For example, a stepmother commented on her young stepdaughter's grief over losing her biological mother to cancer several years earlier. "I miss my mommy," the child muttered softly, as though saying the words out loud was wrong. "I know you miss your mother, and I understand that you are sad," the stepmother told the child. "You can say you miss her out loud." Given permission for the first time in three years to express herself, the girl released pent-up tears and cried for nearly half an hour. Her stepmother's acceptance of her feelings helped this grief-stricken girl to express them. Just a few words helped to stimulate the girl's grieving and ultimately helped her say goodbye to her beloved mother.

In another example of intentional communication, a mother was driving her two teenage daughters to an event and the topic of abortion came up. The mother felt that the topic was so critical that she found a place to park so she could look at the girls face-to-face as they continued the discussion.

Good communication also includes the ability to express thoughts and opinions in an honest, healthy, and assertive way. Adults can teach girls the power of assertiveness and emphasize that disagreeing with someone is fair and may also lead to healthy debate. Healthy assertiveness and conflict resolution both contribute nicely to the flow of communication.

Teaching girls the difference between aggression and assertiveness is done by example and through education. Assertiveness is defined as balancing the rights of others and one's own rights. Assertiveness means having the courage to tell the store clerk that one was shortchanged, to tell a friend she prefers to do something different, to ask for clarification when a message was misunderstood, and to confidently say, "This is what I want and need." Assertive communication is healthy communication.

Interestingly, the ability to express honest feelings and opinions is ultimately the greatest safeguard *against* uncomfortable conflict. Time and time again, in our professional roles as a psychologist and a coach, we work with women who define themselves as assertive but admit they avoid expressing their opinions in situations or with specific personality types for fear of conflict. Contrary to popular sentiment, personal and business relationships can survive honest conflict that is respectfully expressed using an appropriate tone.

Healthy conflict and assertiveness are best expressed face-to-face or verbally on the phone. Is it any surprise that some children have learned to resolve disputes and differences via text messages and online communication? As technology makes our lives more and more convenient, there may be a decline in our ability to solve problems in person. Social scientists estimate that only 7% of communication is verbal.

That means that 93% of what we communicate comes from body language, facial expressions, and delivery. When words are written, the remaining 93% of the communication is absent. Readers are left to interpret messages in their own way.

When texting or social media is used as a primary means of communication, particularly during a conflict, meaning is often lost and resentment builds. Using electronic devices to resolve conflict leaves communication open to assumptions about what the other individual meant. All too often, electronic conflict resolution leads to severed relationships, and the advantages of face-to-face speaking are lost. Verbal conflict resolution enables the speaker and listener to obtain clarification on what was heard. Disagreements may be resolved and the relationship repaired. It also enhances verbal communication skills.

Conflict resolution is a skill. Most relationships at some point will experience conflict, yet nearly half of the women in our survey reported fearing conflict. Even though they did not specify the type of conflict, their desire to avoid it was quite clear. What actions do many take to deal with conflict? Often, it's avoidance, and what follows is separation. This pattern is becoming more commonplace in society. Our girls are learning to "shoot" texts or brief messages back and forth in conflict. Should the girls see one another at school, they may pass without speaking and resume the electronic conflict resolution later.

Direct communication is being replaced by electronic means in many arenas. Parents and teachers primarily communicate by email. College courses may be taken online. Certainly, modern technology has made life convenient, but it doesn't replace the need for direct communication and conflict resolution.

Women and girls need a culture where healthy communication and conflict are not feared. Such a culture begins at home. Communicating with children must extend beyond simple conversations that require "yes" and "no" answers. Asking open-ended questions that require a more detailed response stimulates conversation. One survey respondent suggested that grown-ups "talk to young girls about world affairs or complex political and ethical dilemmas." Girls appreciate parents and caregivers paying close attention to what they think about such issues. They also appreciate adults taking an active interest in their young lives. Body language is also crucial in good communication at home. You can use body language to show the girls in your life that they matter, such as leaning forward, smiling, and regularly lowering your body so you are at her eye level and can maintain eye contact.

Girls emulate their role models and learn through example. They acquire good communication skills when the adults around them communicate well. One woman reported that she was empowered by consistent encouragement to openly express herself during childhood. This same woman describes herself as independent and as having a deep sense of self-respect. When girls are listened to, engaged with, and encouraged in their communication, they have the opportunity to become happier and more fulfilled adults. We need to expect and encourage our girls to have opinions and ask questions.

Suggestions to Encourage Communication:

- Remember that to listen well is to love well. Make sure that when you are listening to her, you are *truly* hearing what she has to say. Good listening is good role modeling. Convey your acceptance and understanding of her messages.

- Focus on open-ended questions that encourage more conversation. For instance, use the words "how," "why," and "tell me more" in conversation.

- Be specific when you ask her questions. Parents often complain that when they ask how their child's day went, they receive little more than a grunt. Instead, ask about the high point of her day. A question like that is more likely to elicit a detailed response.

- Try playing Roses (highs) and Thorns (lows) with her each day. Establishing customs such as this instills a feeling of connection and belonging, and encourages communication.

- Read stories and discuss them afterward.

- Help her to verbally express her feelings as they occur. This is part of emotional intelligence. For instance, a girl who is bullied by a peer feels hurt and sad. We know that. Reflect that feeling back to her. This lets her know she is understood. Say, "You feel sad."

- Take anger out of the correction process. Always let her know that she is loved.

- Model respect toward others and toward your girl. Listen and attend to what she is saying and use respectful language. Respect yourself.

- Respect her opinions without judgment. Also, help her to express those opinions respectfully.

- Read one of the many books on assertiveness and learn to model assertiveness. Embrace the belief that everyone deserves to be assertive, which includes the ability to say what one wants or needs.

- Resist the temptation to openly degrade yourself, particularly in girls' presence. Be aware of your own self-talk.

- Girls need to learn to "toot their own horns." Encourage her to say what she's good at, especially in the workplace when it's time for a raise. Teach her a healthy balance between giving herself credit, conveying self-confidence, and maintaining humility.

No matter what opinions she develops as she grows up, always listen to your girl respectfully, pay attention to her, and let her know you love her, even if you don't love her views. She, in turn, is more likely to develop good listening skills herself if she learns them at home, and to treat others with respect if she is respected herself. Rather than feel guilty over what you believe you need to change, try to be aware of how to improve communication with your daughter and make the changes you—and your children—need. It's healthy to disagree respectfully. As parents or role models, you are constantly setting examples for your children's behaviors. Invest more time in talking to your child about events of the day or making up songs or telling jokes.

◇◇◇◇◇◇◇◇◇◇◇◇

Simply listen to the song, "Just Brave."
—BY SARA BAREILLES

◇◇◇◇◇◇◇◇◇◇◇◇

4

Self-Discipline

"Without discipline there is no life at all."
—KATHERINE HEPBURN

Girls learn self-discipline by being responsible for their behavior. Responsibility is taught and reinforced primarily in the home. Most parents will agree that their daughter needs to learn responsibility, and most girls surely want the benefits that go along with being responsible and self-reliant. Self-discipline is the driving force behind success, competence, joy, self-regulation, happiness, and much more.

For some, being self-disciplined means being well

behaved; for others, it means being self-sufficient. A hallmark of self-discipline is the ability to hold off getting what one wants today in order to gain something more satisfying and rewarding in the future—even if doing so requires effort and time. Those who practice self-discipline often attribute this quality to some of their life lessons learned, successes, and positive self-esteem.

Parents often ask how their daughters became so unwilling to do their chores or do what was asked of them. They wonder why their daughters "demand" certain material items and "refuse" to earn what they want. The answer is often uncomfortably clear. Such self-discipline is lacking because it was never taught. These girls lacked opportunities to be held accountable and become aware of the consequences of their actions. They had not yet experienced the power of earning what they receive.

We know that the process of learning and acquiring self-discipline starts in early childhood. During this time parents teach toddlers to behave safely, warn them to avoid hot stoves and busy streets, and monitor and portion their food. In time, children learn to monitor those behaviors. As language develops, manners, kindness, and sharing are also taught. By the time girls reach their teen years, behavior patterns have been fairly well established. Some are beginning to appreciate the value of hard work in this stage and have learned that through their efforts they may gain the rewards of their accomplishments. Others have learned how to get what they want without the work involved. Teaching them the value of working for what one attains will help them internalize a good work ethic and value their accomplishments. Don't we all remember a time in childhood when we achieved something and felt proud of what we had done?

Parents, in their quest to assist, may lessen the power of their girl's self-determination. Well-meaning adults may try to shield their daughters from emotional hurt or hardship, and through their desire to "fix" what is wrong, may unintentionally take from them the *power of problem-solving*. Girls learn from being encouraged and allowed to solve their own age-appropriate problems.

Parents seeking assistance in correcting their children's problematic behaviors often ask how and why things went wrong. Parents, often well intentioned, unknowingly miss out on opportunities to teach self-discipline. Life lessons are often learned through trial and error, which, at times, involves discomfort for both parents and children! Few children learn from hearing what they should do. Allowing them a chance to practice self-discipline can be effective. For example, prior to getting together with friends, they may be required to do their homework. Routines such as this one allow them to learn the value of self-discipline at an early age so they can continue the practice into their adult lives.

Research suggests punishment is not necessarily an effective means of instilling responsibility. Nagging is easy; however, allowing the children in your life to experience the natural consequences of their actions can teach them self-discipline. Consequences are the master teachers of life! For example, if the child does not finish her homework, she is not allowed to socialize with her friends that night. Likewise, overindulging children leads to major difficulty with acquiring self-discipline. Many parents surveyed admit to spoiling their children out of guilt. By allowing children to experience consequences for their choices, parents help them to modify their own behaviors.

Rudolf Dreikurs, a prominent child psychiatrist, nicely outlines the benefits of natural and logical consequences. Dreikurs explains that children learn to avoid behaviors that bring about uncomfortable consequences. For example, the child who habitually forgets to bring her musical instrument to school might learn to remember if she is allowed to suffer the natural consequences, such as not being able to participate in music class that day.

Each girl is an individual with her own will. However, if children don't learn self-discipline and rules, they may not learn that the time and feelings of others are equally as important as their own immediate needs. Teaching girls self-discipline helps them to respect the needs of others, respect authority, and remain safe. Self-discipline will help them to manage their impulses, make good and safe choices, consider consequences, and think before acting. By demonstrating the importance of both independence and self-discipline, girls are poised for success, both in their work and in their relationships later in life.

By developing self-discipline, girls learn to be accountable for their actions. They enjoy the benefits of independence and learn to rely on their inner resources. The challenge for parents is to help girls find safe ways to gain that sense of accomplishment and independence. As time goes on, girls will find ways to budget their time, complete assignments, fulfill obligations, care for themselves, and make better choices.

Consider these examples:

A mother called a therapist about her teenage girl who was harming herself physically, refusing to complete her homework, and challenging authority. Her daughter would not agree to come for counseling, but her mother was willing to attend sessions. The mother learned that the root of her daughter's problems was the girl's desperate need for discipline. The daughter had not learned to take responsibility for her actions. Instead, she expected her parents to cater to her demands. So her parents established more room for her to learn self-discipline. She earned back the use of her cell phone by paying most of the bill, and she completed her homework before being permitted to socialize with her friends. In a short period of time, and largely through her parents' efforts, she began to take more responsibility for herself.

Some parents complain about spending hours each night helping their children with homework. They usually insist that such time is necessary, fearing their children will fail. When asked who is more invested in the homework, they invariably and reluctantly admit that they are. Once these well-meaning parents expect their children to be responsible for their own homework, the children become more independent.

Suggestions for Teaching Self-Discipline:

* Encourage self-discipline by allowing your child to work diligently at finding her own solutions to age-appropriate problems. Every time she solves a problem independently, she gains another morsel of confidence and courage to solve her next problem.

* Learn about the value of consequences; embrace opportunities to watch your daughter learn from them. Talk about the lesson learned.

* Try to better understand your desire to shield her from the very discomfort that will help her learn and mature.

* Model patience and the ability to delay gratification. Avoid knee-jerk reactions and manage your impulses.

- Respect your daughter's (safe) choices even if you disagree with them, such as allowing her to experiment with her choice of clothing.

- Help her to reflect on her behaviors to increase her self-awareness. Ask, "How did that work out for you?"

- Talk openly with your daughter about your own challenges with delaying gratification.

- Teach your daughter that dreaming is one part of becoming who she wants to be, and that effort is needed to realize her dreams.

- Value manners as important behaviors to be taught and practiced in and out of the home.

- Help her praise herself for successfully dealing with a difficult situation in a calm, sensible way. "You are so pleased that you completed your report on time."

- Teach her about discipline with finances, purchases, savings, banking, etc.

- Remember, dessert follows dinner. Pleasure follows effort.

◇◇◇◇◇◇◇◇◇◇◇◇

"The first and best victory is to conquer self."

—PLATO

◇◇◇◇◇◇◇◇◇◇◇◇

5

Independence

*"Give a [wo]man a fish and she will eat for a day;
teach [her] to fish and [s]he will eat for a lifetime."*
—A CHINESE PROVERB

Independence has many faces: a three-year-old insisting on figuring out how to put her coat on her way; children who complete their homework independently without parental assistance; or girls who choose careers based on their own expressed interests. While independence is an important skill for any young child to learn, independence is a critical skill for girls and women because girls aren't often given the opportunity to learn independence in the same way that boys are. While many boys are ingrained with the knowledge that they can and should be independent, girls often aren't expected to do things on their own or solve their own problems in quite the same way. Because of this, we may need to be extra careful that we are checking our biases and instilling lessons of independence in our daughters as well as our sons.

It is less important to set ironclad rules that spell out exactly how and when a girl is granted the privileges of independence. It is more important that she be encouraged to embrace the spirit of independence. Consider the quote at the beginning of this chapter. If we teach a girl that she holds the key to self-sufficiency, she will learn to embrace many opportunities to do things for herself. A girl will approach new situations with a healthy curiosity. In turn, she will acquire a sense of satisfaction and gain self-esteem.

In our work, we encounter many young girls and parents who come to the counselor's office with the notion that the therapist will "fix" the daughter's "problem." One mother who came to counseling noted that she had given the girl "all she wanted." But when her daughter no longer respected her or her rules and refused to do what was asked of her, the mother sought help. She asked that the therapist try to change her daughter's attitude.

The mother was surprised by the suggestion that she, alone, could effect change far more efficiently by changing her expectations of her daughter. Rather than doing things for her daughter, the mother could teach the girl independence by insisting she learn to take care of herself and practice responsible behaviors. In time, the daughter's respect for her mother improved, and she was taking more initiative to care for herself.

Another woman's single mother prepared her for life with uncanny foresight by allowing her to experience age-appropriate independence as a child. Some may have considered her expectations of her daughter a bit demanding, but when this mother died while her daughter was a young adult, the daughter was able to practice the life skills her mother had taught her. Even though she was not emotionally prepared for the loss of her mother, she became an incredibly independent woman.

In her book *Bringing Up Bébé: One American Mother Discovers the Wisdom of French Parenting,* author Pamela Druckerman marvels at French parents who naturally encourage independence in their children while also enforcing clear limits and rules. According to Druckerman, parents in France are far less likely to hover over their children while they play or complete chores. Instead, the children understand their responsibilities and learn to internalize guidelines for their own behavior.

Play therapy is frequently used as a means for helping children work through problems symbolically. The therapist may take a nondirective role and thus allow the child to work through solving a problem on her own. The therapist will not intervene to help the child unless her help is requested. During play therapy, children often work hard to do things like figure out how to open something, learn to successfully build a structure, or learn how to work a cash register. Once the child figures out how to solve the problem, she experiences a marvelous feeling of accomplishment. Also, her resilience is fortified. The therapist then reflects to the child a feeling of happiness or pride.

If a child is struggling with something, and an adult kindly intervenes to assist, the problem is frequently solved but the child's confidence is diminished. She is likely to assume that the adult is all-knowing and that she, the child, is incompetent. If, instead, a child attempts a task and finally succeeds after repeated efforts, she gains a great sense of accomplishment. Even if she is unsuccessful and eventually asks for help, she learns that help is available if she truly needs it. Children who request help certainly deserve assistance after first trying to solve problems themselves. In asking for help, they are also using their assertiveness skills!

Girls truly appreciate attention to, and support for, their chosen interests and activities. Such support helps them develop the confidence needed to pursue their interests. And this very support is infinitely valuable. It's difficult, but parents must stand back and let their girls learn skills in their own time. Girls must be allowed to make mistakes and understand that doing so is not the end of the world! Mistakes are a part of life. Girls will take their cues from Mom and Dad when accidents or mistakes occur. If parents are relaxed about them, their daughters will be, too. All children learn and gain confidence by doing. They cannot be expected to do things perfectly. When things go wrong they need to develop the courage to try again. Poet Maya Angelou once said in an interview that courage is the greatest virtue; and we believe it leads to independence.

Sometimes children receive mixed messages about where and when they should exert independence. For example, two parents came to counseling to discuss their daughter's unmanageable behaviors and did not understand how to grant appropriate levels of independence to her. Although the parents gave their 14-year-old girl the freedom to be in a sexual relationship with a 16-year-old-boyfriend, they kept her dependent on them by giving in to her demand that they order her food in restaurants. They meant to be helpful yet inadvertently were giving her a mixed message about the areas in which she truly needed to exert independence. It appeared that the girl was old enough to be in a sexual relationship but too young to order her own food.

If one could be guaranteed a lifetime of dependence on someone else, there would be no need for independence. But there is no such guarantee for anyone. Only one thing is certain: that girls who learn to become independent rather than dependent will experience self-confidence, courage, and authenticity, and develop resiliency muscles. Allowing girls to become independent means granting them the latitude to solve their own problems, do their own homework, and take responsibility for the consequences of their behaviors. Both dependence and independence are learned.

Many of our respondents noted that as children they were not encouraged to be independent and to establish their own unique identities. Many worked excruciatingly hard to overcome the effects of such an upbringing to gain more independence as adults. It is difficult to decide when to intervene and when to allow our children to work through problems on their own. In most situations, it is about trusting that they have the resources to handle their problems as you remain ready and willing to intervene if the situation becomes too overwhelming.

Suggestions for Encouraging Independence:

- Equip her with the gift of ongoing curiosity by asking her questions and encouraging and appreciating the questions she asks.

- Model a good relationship with yourself.

- Provide clear rules and structure while allowing her the freedom to explore her dreams.

- Barring safety issues, allow her to attempt to find answers and to attempt new tasks.

- Allow her to experience the sometimes awkward process of learning new skills rather than intervening to do things for her.

- Encourage her to cook, pack her own lunches, use age-appropriate tools, become involved in sports, or run for school office.

- Teach her about finances, from her piggy bank to her own bank account.

- Set an example; be a risk taker. Try something new.

- Model self-satisfaction, e.g., "I feel great after I exercise."

- Take off the training wheels and watch her go!

✧✧✧✧✧✧✧✧✧✧✧✧

"Feel the fear and do it anyway!"
—SUSAN JEFFERS

✧✧✧✧✧✧✧✧✧✧✧✧

6

Nurturance / Self-Care

*"If our children are to approve of themselves . . .
they must see we approve of ourselves."*
—Maya Angelou

Women are notorious for their caretaking abilities, often excelling in reaching out to those in need while placing their own needs on the back burner. The challenge for women and girls lies in finding a balance between caring for self and others. Our survey respondents revealed a need for more instruction in this area. They realized that self-care can be done at any age but wished they would have been introduced to it much earlier. Some noted that if they had paid more attention to their own care, they would have been more prepared and fulfilled earlier in life.

We propose that nurturance involves exquisite self-care! Girls can learn to take good care of themselves at any age. And the better care they learn early on, the better they feel, the healthier life choices they make, and the deeper self-respect they gain. Good habits established during childhood continue into adulthood.

Sometimes girls are unprepared to self-nurture until they are able to draw from past experiences of nurturance. We are accustomed to looking to mothers as a sole source of role modeling; however, multiple other potential sources of inspiration exist. Outside sources of nurturance tend to trickle into girls' lives in the form of caring teachers, a friend's mother, or a significant female in their lives. Frequently, those sources are more abundant than one realizes.

We encourage women and girls to look beyond their immediate family for sources of nurturance during the formative years. Those who wish to further explore sources of their own nurturing have derived much benefit from a favorite book, *Mothering Ourselves* by Evelyn Bassoff.

The reader realizes that the ability to celebrate the overlooked positive influences in one's life is a start to gaining the ability to self-nurture.

You can influence the girls you love to take responsibility for their self-care in any or all of these areas of development:

Physical—Many organizations, such as Girls on the Run, one of our favorites, encourage physical fitness and help participants develop self-respect and healthy lifestyle choices. Being a part of an organization like this, or engaging in other types of regular physical activity, teaches girls to take care of and respect their bodies, brains, and lives. Physical activity also gives one a sense of achievement.

- Focus on fitness rather than on body image.

- Exercise is critical to a sense of well-being. Encourage physical over sedentary activity. Remind her that physical activity breeds energy and sedentary activity breeds inactivity.

- Set examples for good personal hygiene. Showers, brushing teeth, brushing hair, and clean clothes give a girl a feeling of refreshment.

- Posture can also have an effect on physical and mental well-being. Encourage her to walk tall with shoulders back and head held high. This will improve her self-confidence.

- Model and motivate healthy eating and adequate sleep.

- Have on hand healthy, whole-food snacks such as fresh fruits and vegetables or snacks low in sugar.

- Model drinking plenty of fresh water.

- Encourage her to simply think about a cheerful event and smile.

- Encourage natural and practical solutions to daily discomforts, such as headaches, when possible. For example, model deep breathing, taking walks, sitting in nature, and other natural solutions to de-stress.

- Teach her to practice age-appropriate affirmations on how to listen to her body. Suggest she look in the mirror as she makes these self-statements: "I know how to love myself." "I appreciate my body's wisdom." "I trust my body to guide me." "My body is a fabulous machine." "I really like me."

Sexual—Sexuality exists at birth and is important to a girl's healthy functioning. Parents are generally advised to have the traditional conversation about sexuality when their children are approaching adolescence; however, education may begin from the start. Treating your girl's sexuality as natural eliminates shame and helps her to seek out answers to questions from a healthy adult. In turn, she is more likely to take care of herself in sexual relationships.

- Refer to body parts using their appropriate terms.

- Encourage positive references to bodies.

- Teach her to cherish her body and make informed sexual choices.

- Share books about girls' sexual health and encourage conversations about them.

- Offer age-appropriate responses to questions about sexuality.

- Remain receptive to frequent conversations about sexuality.

- Encourage conversation about sexually provocative messages from the media and what she believes is being conveyed. Help her to understand the intent behind the messages.

- Comment on billboards that have hidden sexual messages.

- Read with your girl.

Emotional—Emotional health stems from the ability to identify and express feelings as they occur. This ability to express and understand feelings in their purest form helps with problem-solving throughout the life span. In turn, relationships and life choices are based on solid self-awareness. When a child experiences a feeling and that feeling is reflected, the child feels nurtured and in turn develops the internal ability to recognize her feelings. When children attend play therapy, the therapist reflects their feelings while they occur. This is an ideal way to teach children how to take care of their emotions. For example, the therapist may say, "Oh, you feel so proud of that!" The child learns to recognize that what she is feeling at that exact moment is pride.

Just as children need to use their muscles to keep them moving, emotional muscle is needed for children to learn trust and adaptability, and to thrive. Communication, talking with children, and listening to them helps children to develop empathy and learn confidence. In turn, cooperation and competence develop. Thus, a child's mental health is crucial to her development. If we remain aware of her emotional health, we can lead her to develop strong emotional muscle.

* Practice reflecting your girl's feelings back to her. Worry less about being accurate and more about showing an interest in understanding her. This is an excellent way to nurture.

* Show your interest in what she is saying by looking her directly in the eyes.

* If she is struggling with a concern, remember that internal conflicts and discomfort often lead to personal emotional growth. Listen to her and reflect her feelings. Help her to say what she wants to say, and let her find her own solutions.

* Be aware of her self-talk, the messages she tells herself. If she says, "I did a horrible job in the game," reframe her statement: "You are learning new skills and improving."

* Talk about empathy, what it means and how it feels. Empathy involves the ability to understand and share the feelings of others.

- Have her congratulate herself when she is pleased with something she has done.

- Free play is crucial to the development of emotional stability, persistence, problem-solving, and social etiquette. Incorporate free play into family life. Many happy memories arise out of family fun.

- Listen to music, sing loudly, and help her to relax.

- Seek mental health services before situations become unmanageable. Pursue counseling as readily as you would make a doctor's appointment. Emotional health is equally important; help to nurture it!

Relational—We need to be aware of how our children play and interact and what messages they are giving and receiving. Talking to them about their interactions, asking lots of questions, and offering feedback on their perceptions help them to understand the value of relationships. Suggestions and guidance are often necessary. Like adults, children tend to fare better in relationships when they are able to talk through problems. Healthy relationships are another form of nurturance for girls. Girls and women seek out conversation as a source of nurturance.

One of our friends plays Roses and Thorns with her children before bed—an incredibly nurturing activity. The kids tell her some of the best (roses) and worst (thorns) parts of their day. In turn, they are learning that their perspectives and feelings are important. They are learning to listen to one another and reciprocate in relationships. Such experiences help children develop conversational skills that may later help them navigate relationships. They are learning that they have a voice and are given credibility. Further, they learn to be comfortable in social settings and to show an interest in others. It is confidence in one's ability to relate to others that helps young girls think ahead to a future with a leadership role if they choose. And it is the ability to reciprocate in relationships that teaches girls to negotiate, to make good decisions, and to work harmoniously with upper management in their careers.

- Listen to her by fully attending to what she is saying and by responding so that she learns to do the same in relationships.

- Go beyond asking, "How was school?," and instead ask something more specific. "What did you do in math class today?" This will encourage more meaningful conversation and convey interest.

- Play the "favorite" game, which many children enjoy. Take turns naming favorite sports, ice cream flavors, days of the week, or ways to celebrate birthdays. Such exchanges help her to discover herself.

- Set the cell phone aside and remind yourself that no technology is needed to cultivate a warm and meaningful relationship with her.

- Encourage her to solve interpersonal problems by talking rather than texting.

- Remain alert to family and peer bullying. Learn more about bullying and ways to empower her to stand up for herself and her friends, when possible.

- Model honesty in your relationships.

- Model assertiveness in your relationships.

- Openly express affection. Younger girls like to share affection with loved ones.

Intellectual—Healthy parenting helps girls develop the ability to think critically. Critical thinking includes a number of skills that helps girls learn to make decisions. It helps them evaluate information to determine whether it is right or wrong. To think critically about a problem or issue means to be open-minded and able to view alternative ways of looking at solutions. Children with good critical thinking skills will eventually learn to make necessary decisions independent of their parents. Further, critical thinking can help her choose a meaningful career.

- Accept her views whether you agree with them or not. Show respect!

- Make thinking fun by playing intellectually stimulating games or encouraging a love of books.

- Pursue knowledge through curiosity. Ask questions and seek answers together.

- Engage in educational activities during the summer or during long school breaks.

- Encourage self-expression as a means of learning about life and relationships.

- Visit museums.

- Go on walks and identify trees, flowers, and birds.

- Ask her who she wants to be when she grows up.

- Celebrate choices children make even if you are not in agreement, such as offbeat hairstyle, clothing choices, or unusual interests.

- Teach critical thinking by looking deeper into information presented. Ask questions!

- Capture teachable moments!

- Embrace the challenge of cultivating your girl's intellect.

- Help and encourage her to think and ask questions.

- Honor her feelings and help her examine why she feels what she does.

- Teach her to rely on her mind to make decisions and nurture her intellect.

Spiritual—People find nurturance through spirituality. Some may do so through organized religion, others through practicing yoga or being in nature.

However it is practiced, spirituality is important because it defines how she views the universe and sees herself in relation to the world. It is a great source of internal nurturance and encompasses her deepest values and the meanings by which she lives. Spirituality develops and changes over time; usually it's influenced by poignant life experiences. You, the influencer, can cultivate those experiences.

- Talk to the girl you love about meaningful topics.

- Talk about emotional safety and try to create a safe environment for her to find peace.

- Encourage her to delve deeply into topics that interest her.

- Help her to value her life and nature.

- Intentionally recognize what you are grateful for and say it out loud!

- Encourage her to create sacred space where she may meditate or sit in silence.

- Teach her that we all face adversity and that it is not the event but how we react to it that will determine the joy and happiness in our lives.

- Teach empathy whenever possible.

- Model your own ability to experience pleasure and joy.

- Expose her to music as a means of self-soothing. Try drumming!

- Help her to see the glass as half-full.

- Be gentle with yourself and make time for self-care. Take a walk, sit and drink a cup of tea, or soak in the tub.

"Music was my refuge. I could crawl into the space between the notes and curl my back to loneliness."

—MAYA ANGELOU

7

Boundaries

"Daring to set boundaries is about having the courage to love ourselves, even when we risk disappointing others."
—BRENE BROWN, PhD

Boundaries are familiar to us in many aspects of our lives. For example, our home is considered ours and we hope others respect this designated area. Boundaries are required in most settings and institutions. Large buildings have separate floors, schools have rules, and people have roles. Those types of boundaries are relatively clear and understandable.

Likewise, children have routines and rules, and parents, for the most part, are responsible for ensuring their children follow them. These expectations are also boundaries that distinguish parents from children. Our concern, though, is that boundaries seem blurred and are becoming less and less obvious in modern parenting. While some parents clearly define boundaries to their children, some well-meaning parents tend to doubt their own authority and give in to the protesting child. They may avoid setting needed limits for fear of disappointing their child or of having to deal with dreaded opposition.

Although we certainly don't advocate returning to the old days of children being seen and not heard, we can surely talk about clear distinctions between parents and children. Counselors often do so after parents consult with them about their children's behavioral problems. The parents may complain about their children's "unwillingness" to complete chores or respect their authority. Those parents may admit to having often resisted establishing clear rules. When their children failed to adhere to a rule or complete a chore, the tendency was to do some of their own protesting, argue with the child to do the chore, and eventually surrender to the child's will.

Some of the benefits of having strong and clear

boundaries with children are obvious. For example, the child who grows up with rules and limits tends to respect authority outside of the home, at school, at work, etc. Further, the child with clear boundaries tends to feel secure.

Boundaries in the parent-child relationship go beyond setting rules and sticking to them. Girls have a strong need for fairness and understanding. Girls love to talk, so giving them the opportunity to discuss the purpose of certain rules may lead to greater coop-eration. Certain rules are clearly non-negotiable; how-ever, giving them the benefit of understanding why will encourage a more cooperative relationship.

Talking about rules differs from engaging in nego-tiation about rules, a tactic frequently used by children (and some adults!) to get their way. Often, daughters and parents have made their way to the therapy room due to their inability to get along. Some teenage girls and their parents engage in debates over what the girls should or should not do. Their parents may wonder how they reached such an impasse. Interestingly, the parents and children have actually reversed roles, with the daughter demanding certain rights and the par-ents defending their position. This type of exchange differs from one that involves explaining rules. Here, she hopes her protests may lead to her desired end, a change in rules. The boundaries have been blurred and the roles have reversed. Granted, these outcomes may be extreme, but they are also becoming quite common.

Parents are on the front line of modeling healthy boundaries in relationships. They are also in a good position to demonstrate strong parent-child boundaries. Those who set limits and allow some choices within those boundaries model self-respect. That is, they convey to their children the value of discipline and respect toward others. Such modeling is particularly important to young girls, who will later need such skills in relationships.

Girls especially need clear boundaries early in life. The girl who learns to abide by adult guidance is also learning how to set limits in her own relationships as she grows up. It's hard to believe healthy discipline can have such a direct relationship to a girl's self-respect and safety. Conversely, girls are often not supported when they express assertiveness, which may leave them feeling vulnerable and like they always need to say yes instead of sticking up for themselves. In all aspects of life—romantic, professional, friendship, and family—it is important to learn how to say no when someone is crossing a line. Because this can be challenging to girls, it's important to teach them how to say no and how to express clear boundaries. Children need to learn how to self-protect.

Assertiveness is one such example of self-protection and personal boundaries. Girls and women often need help with overcoming barriers to assertiveness. They may doubt they have the right to express themselves directly and honestly. They may fear being assertive will create conflict or they may simply lack the skills to express themselves effectively. Confronted with difficult situations, plenty of people respond either aggressively or passively and, in turn, avoid setting boundaries. These responses lead to broken relationships, anxiety, and even physical problems. Assertiveness in females was for many centuries devalued, but now assertive women are far more valued by men, other women, and society. Even so, it is still a challenge for girls and women to express assertiveness. Therefore, it is important to not only teach this skill but practice assertiveness in our own lives so that we may set an example and be a role model for girls to look up to. By cultivating assertiveness in our girls, we can help them reduce stress and increase their sense of worth as females.

Suggestions for Teaching Boundaries:

* Use an adult tone when setting limits. Avoid adding taglines at the end of direct requests such as "OK?"

* Expect respect. Have her practice responding to you in a respectful tone. Model good boundaries by speaking to her and others calmly and respectfully.

* Reflect a feeling of pride or happiness when she has a difficult time behaving but does so anyway. Say, "That was difficult for you, but you feel good about yourself for doing the right thing."

* Teach good boundaries by explaining the consequences of behavior. For example, rather than saying, "Don't do that," it is best to explain, "By doing ____, ____ will happen."

* Keep a schedule that includes regular meal times, chores, and bedtimes.

- Teach her early on about setting boundaries with her own body. Allow her the freedom to reject affection from others or from people with whom she is not comfortable. An excellent resource for parents wanting more information about keeping children safe is *Protecting the Gift* by Gavin de Becker.

- Respect her privacy by allowing her independent time behind closed doors. Close your own door when engaging in private activity.

- Insist she show respect to adults in the community including neighbors, family, friends, and those she meets at church or sports events.

- Grant her some independence when she plays either informal games in the neighborhood or organized team sports. Parents don't need to attend every team practice or intervene when coaches don't do as they want. (Remember, the coach is the authority figure in organized sports, and often respecting the coach's authority is more important than proving him or her wrong.)

* Model clear boundaries in your dealings with others. You are her greatest teacher!

Suggestions for Teaching Assertiveness:

* Recognize your own assertive, aggressive, and passive behaviors and take steps toward modeling assertiveness. (Assertiveness is not aggression.)

* Explain the importance of eye contact for conveying sincerity.

* Be alert to body posture; face others while talking; keep shoulders back.

* Effective assertiveness requires facial expressions that match the feeling. For instance, teach her to refrain from smiling

when angry. Friendliness should be conveyed with a smile.

- Assertiveness includes respect for the rights and feelings of others. Listening well is a critical component of assertiveness. It demonstrates respect for the other person.

- Teach her to express herself and take responsibility for her feelings.

- The style of her delivery is as important as her words. Help her say, "I am angry" or "I would rather. . . ." When the time comes for her to be assertive, she'll have practice with the language.

"'No' is a complete sentence!"
—ANNE LAMOTT

8

Humor

"I don't trust anyone who doesn't laugh."
—MAYA ANGELOU

We would like to make one thing perfectly clear: We love to laugh. We laughed as we discussed the contents of this book and whether it would ever be completed. We laughed at our mistakes. We found humor in the antics of little children who challenged their mothers as they lovingly shared meals at the café where we worked on this book.

We talked about how humor helped us through childhood challenges, and how even during times of sadness we held on to humor as a dear friend. We decided that humor in a person's life is too necessary to be ignored!

We obviously are not alone in our thinking. Several of our survey respondents listed humor as their greatest attribute. Many others said they use humor as a stress reliever. People like humor because they like to feel good. Children love to giggle just for the sake of giggling.

We know from a scientific standpoint that when a person laughs, chemicals in the brain—endorphins—are released. Endorphins make people feel good. They promote an overall sense of well-being and can even temporarily relieve pain.

Laughing and forgetting your troubles can relieve physical tension and lower stress levels. Laughter relaxes the entire body. A good, hearty laugh leaves muscles relaxed for up to 45 minutes.

Laughter helps to maintain long-term friendships. Laughter also builds intimacy. So what better gift than permission to laugh, to find humor in difficult times, and to distract yourself when all else fails?

We recognize, of course, that laughter is not always a solution to life's ills, but we certainly are aware that more of it is needed. Girls need to laugh. Jokes, riddles, and humor help to develop abstract thinking. And the ability to use this higher-level thinking goes hand-in-hand with problem-solving skills.

Laughter does many wonderful things for us. It can:

- Increase immune cells and infection-fighting antibodies, thus improving resistance to disease.

- Boost the immune system and decrease stress hormones.

- Trigger the release of endorphins, the body's natural feel-good chemicals.

- Protect the heart.

- Improve the function of blood vessels and increase blood flow, which can help protect against heart attack and other cardiovascular problems.

As girls mature, some tend to laugh less. As a result, they produce less and less of the chemicals that help to relieve stress and lower the risk of heart attack. One study estimated that the average four-year-old laughs 300 times a day whereas the average 40-year-old laughs only four times a day. More than 60% of adults smile fewer than 20 times a day at home and break into a grin even less often at work. We are smiling and laughing less as a society than we did in the 1950s (Gerloff 2011).

The good news is that there are no laws banning laughter or preventing us from promoting humor. But to share more laughter in your life, it's best to be face-to-face with another person. Joy can be attained by sharing a good laugh with those in our lives however near or far away.

Suggestions for Incorporating Humor:

- Tell her jokes.

- Listen to her jokes.

- Allow time for silliness, such as playing dress-up or other imaginative games.

- Read funny books to her.

- Take her to a funny show.

- Laugh over silly things you say and do together.

- Value humor as a vital and critical element of your girl's existence.

- Help her to learn to laugh at herself. Let her safely say, "I made a mistake."

- Use humor lovingly; avoid using it at the expense of others.

- Practice using humor in your daily routine.

- Ask each other what the funniest thing was that happened today.

- Have fun looking for joke books at your local library or bookstore.

- Incorporate laughter into your day as a regular occurrence, and watch your daughter do the same!

⬦⬦⬦⬦⬦⬦⬦⬦⬦⬦

"I am constantly amazed by Tina Fey, and I am Tina Fey."

—TINA FEY

⬦⬦⬦⬦⬦⬦⬦⬦⬦⬦

9

Friendship

"Peaceful companionship. How blest I am."
—Louise Hay

Kindergarten children may define a friend as someone who "plays with me at recess." Two 12-year-old girls in our lives called a friend "someone you can rely on and trust" and who is "loyal and nice." Friends are food for the soul. What would life be without friends?

A friend is someone you know, like, feel comfortable with, and trust. She is someone with whom you share your feelings and call on when you want to play, sing, or dance.

Friends help girls to grow, evolve, gain self-knowledge, practice problem-solving, develop emotional bonds, learn to give and take, and learn to feel for others—to develop empathy. Friends also help the girls in your life to feel accepted and important, and in turn may help them learn how to practice tolerance and acceptance of others. They build memories with them through shared interests and experiences. Often, friends become the constants in one's life. When we see a good friend after a long separation, we are able to seamlessly pick up where we left off. We tend to cherish the pleasure we derive from such experiences. To stay in the moment is such an added benefit in this modern world, and what better way to stay in the moment than to spend time with a friend? Simply to enjoy!

Learning how to be a good friend starts at an early age. The kindergartner that appreciates the girl who plays with her at recess is already learning the value and importance of friendships. While her parents, mentors, and older children demonstrate relationship skills in their own friendships, she will likely notice the joy and gratitude you derive from friendships, and aspire to have the same in her life.

Girls gain a strong foundation for friendships by learning kind and caring behaviors. Adults who demonstrate kindness, caring, and empathy toward others help to build that important foundation for the girls in their lives. In turn, girls tend to emulate those positive behaviors. For instance, children may be encouraged to hold the door for someone or pick up a dropped item for another person. Women may offer kind gestures toward a mother juggling her groceries, children, and car seats. Such actions speak volumes!

Empathy is a wonderful virtue to acquire and is critical to developing meaningful and fulfilled relationships. Friendships tend to be long-lasting when empathy is conveyed. After all, women often express their love for friends who are available to offer support and a listening ear during times of need.

Just as empathy is needed in friendships, so is the ability to work through conflict. At times girls may have a strong need to process their feelings, particularly when dealing with disagreements. If responsible adults guide girls through the process of understanding a friend's point of view during or after a conflict, girls may gain more insight into their friend's perspective. Such discussions help girls to realize that having different opinions is acceptable in a friendship.

As we wrote this book, we frequently returned to our pressing concern that as time goes on, girls and women will need to make a concerted effort to maintain friendships. Social media now has the advantage of enabling people to foster and maintain many more friendships than older and more direct forms of communication. Unfortunately, sometimes the depth of communication suffers when direct human contact is missing. Technology, while necessary in many ways, is replacing the very valuable experiences of eye contact, a friend's smile, human touch, the sound of her voice, and nonverbal messages. Cell phones and computers can rob people of the positive feelings that can be generated by spending time together.

With technology being readily available, many of us, especially young people, are replacing human contact with social networking. When interpersonal conflicts are expressed in texts or tweets rather than in person, young girls miss out on opportunities to be *appropriately assertive* and resolve conflicts in a healthy manner. Girls may be encouraged to sit down face-to-face to discuss the issue or at least make a phone call.

While we can connect to others faster than ever, we are losing the quality of those connections with others. In restaurants and in homes, people sit at the dinner table immersed in their phones, often busy texting and avoiding direct conversation. Direct contact and face-to-face conversation will always be wonderful things to experience. When we're with friends it's comforting to hear their voices and be in an environment with people who care about us. One of life's simple joys is having great friends that can last for many years. By encouraging budding friendships in the girls in your life, you are teaching them important skills of communication, trust, and conflict management, while allowing them one of the best pleasures in life: spending time with friends.

Suggestions for Helping Her to Cultivate Friendships:

* Allow your daughter to witness the benefits of your cherished friendships.

* Help her to resolve differences with friends through conversation and problem-solving.

- Point out how another person may feel in a particular circumstance to help her develop empathy, an important component in friendships.

- Equip your home with games and activities that teach empathy and sensitivity toward others, e.g., the Ungame.

- Try to have weekly conversations that elicit compassion toward others.

- Talk frequently about the importance and value of friendships.

- Challenge her when she talks about getting along better with boys than girls. This remark is frequently made by girls who are avoiding working through girl problems!

- Organize play dates to foster friendships between both children and their parents.

- Pay close attention to how a young girl interacts with her friends; ask her to share her thoughts about those relationships.

- Encourage her to treat friends with respect and to honor her commitments. If she makes plans with a friend, help her to understand the importance of keeping those plans rather than changing them for something "better" that comes along.

- Monitor her use of social networks early on. Teach her how to use social media responsibly.

- Encourage phone calls or direct contact over emailing or texting.

- Remember, you set the example for how to be a good friend. No technology needed!

"Friends are my estate."
—EMILY DICKINSON

Conclusion: Listen to the Women

Today's young females are both vulnerable and blessed. They are susceptible to many negative messages through the media, which is an ever-present influence. They are often spending less time with adults who could help to compensate for those messages. Beauty, body shapes, and Botox are dictating the media's messages, and these have a powerful influence.

Fortunately, today's girls are also blessed with greater access to information and knowledge. Their parents, relatives, and role models are becoming more attuned to how to help them develop into competent and confident females. Women, in general, now are more aware of the power of assertiveness, self-care, critical thinking, authenticity, nurturance, and their own spiritual journeys. Despite these advances, women continue to occupy a small portion of jobs in filmmaking, government, management, and other sectors, and still earn only 78 cents to the dollar that men earn. And many women still unknowingly embrace long-held myths about their capabilities.

We believe that by *mindfully* implementing a few ideas from this book in your daily life, you will make significant positive changes in your world and in the girls in your life.

After gathering information from many sources, including surveys and interviews from more than 1,000 women and from people working in various organizations for the betterment of women, one truth is clear: You can have a tremendous influence over how girls look at the world and themselves. You can make this impact with relatively little effort. We encourage you to look at what others are doing to impact girls' development in positive ways and join their effort! Encourage the girls in your life to take advantage of the many new and exciting opportunities available to them in sports, education, careers, and technology.

Consider what we and our respondents shared with your girls. Allow these insights to inform your *intentional* interactions with your most prized possessions: your girls, your daughters, your nieces, your friends' daughters, your granddaughters, and your students. May all girls and women know how amazingly magnificent they are and not allow others to thwart their power.

Girls and women deserve and need to love and respect themselves now! Self-respect is a feeling conveyed to others and often is given back. When everyone respects girls and women, the world will be a better place. Imagine this and live into it!

We trust that you have been inspired by the ideas you read in this book to model and teach courage, confidence, and authenticity. And may you and the girls in your life know how . . .

AMAZINGLY MAGNIFICENT
YOU & THEY TRULY ARE!!!

◇◇◇◇◇◇◇◇◇◇◇

"Surviving is important. Thriving is elegant."
—MAYA ANGELOU

◇◇◇◇◇◇◇◇◇◇◇

Sources Cited

Catalyst, a New York-based nonprofit organization working to accelerate progress for women in the workplace.

Center for American Women and Politics, Rutgers University, Eagleton Institute of Politics.

Gerloff, Pamela. June 21, 2011, "You're not laughing enough, and that's no joke." *Psychology Today.*

Lindzon, Jared. August 26, 2015, "On our 95th Women's Equality Day, women are still waiting for equal treatment." *Fortune.* See http://statusofwomendata.org.

Miss Representation. Dir. Jennifer Siebel Newsom. Girls' Club Entertainment, 2011. Film.

Racine, Hope. June 24, 2015, "Differences in men's and women's salaries in sports show female athletes experience the wage gap too." See www.bustle.com.

"Real girls, real pressure: A national report on the state of self-esteem," June 2008. Dove Self-Esteem Fund.

Advocacy Organizations for Girls and Women

Girls on the Run
Girls Leadership Institute
Girls For a Change
The Representation Project
Young Women Empowered
The Diller-von Furstenberg Family Foundation
Girl Scouts of America
Girl Talk, Inc.
Girls Inc.
Hu-MAN Up
Groove With Me—Dancing to a Positive Future

Composed by North Market Street Graphics
Lancaster, Pennsylvania

Designed by Mark Righter